More Microwave Magic

Edited by Wendy Lazor

Modern Publishing
A Division of Unisystems, Inc.
New York, New York 10022

Printed in the U.S.A.

INTRODUCTION

Use any one of the sixteen carefully selected titles in the easy-to-read **Convenient Cooking**™ series to prepare simple or exotic meals, to learn new culinary skills or to enhance those you already have.

Learn to bake cakes in your microwave, prepare delicious meals with vegetables, or tantalizing low calorie recipes complete with calorie count for each portion. Contemplate dozens of new ideas for lunches and snacks, wake up your tastebuds with Cajun cooking, or follow any of the easy baking recipes for luscious pies and cakes. You can have a hearty meal in minutes or receive raves for making your own fresh pasta.

From appetizers to desserts, you will be delighted with the recipes in the **Convenient Cooking**™ series, the only series any cook really needs.

Welcome to the family of **Convenient Cooking**™.

BARBECUED WINGS

Ingredients:

1 tablespoon margarine
1/4 cup onion, minced
1 clove garlic, minced
1 cup catsup
2 tablespoons brown
   sugar
1/4 cup vinegar
1 teaspoon dry mustard
1 teaspoon hot sauce
1 pound chicken wings,
   tips cut off

Directions:

Put margarine, onion and garlic in a medium-sized microwave-safe baking dish. Cook on HIGH for 2 minutes or until onion is tender. Add catsup, sugar, vinegar, mustard and hot sauce, mix well. Microwave on HIGH for 2 minutes, stirring once during cooking time. Remove from microwave. Place chicken wings on glass pie plate, placing thicker parts toward the outside of the plate. Brush with catsup mixture. Cover with waxed paper. Microwave on HIGH for 10 minutes. Turn wings over and brush with catsup mixture, rotate plate 1/4 turn. Cook on HIGH for 8 minutes or until wings are fully cooked. Serve with any extra catsup sauce.

Yield: 4 servings
Preparation time: 30 minutes

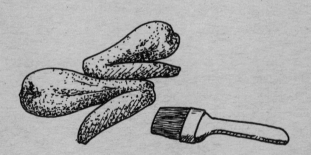

BEANY DIP

Ingredients:

- 1 (8-ounce) can chili hot beans
- 1 cup Monterey Jack cheese
- 1 (16-ounce) can tomatoes
- 1/4 cup Jalapeño peppers, chopped
- Tortilla chips

Directions:

Combine beans, cheese, tomatoes and peppers in a 2-quart microwave-safe casserole dish. Mix well. Cover, cook on HIGH for 3 minutes until heated thoroughly, stir once during cooking. Remove from microwave, stir. Serve warm with tortilla chips.

Yield: 3 cups
Preparation time: 15 minutes

BEEF NACHOS

Ingredients:

1 pound lean ground beef
1/4 cup onion, minced
1 teaspoon cumin
1 (8-ounce) package tortilla chips
1 cup Cheddar cheese, shredded
1 cup Monterey Jack cheese, shredded
1/4 cup olives
1/4 cup sour cream

Directions:

Place ground beef, onion and cumin in a 2-quart microwave-safe casserole dish. Cook on HIGH for 5 minutes or until heated through, stir several times while cooking. Remove from oven and drain. Arrange chips on a microwave-safe serving plate. Top with ground beef mixture, cheeses and olives. Cook on LOW heat until cheese is melted, about 2 minutes. Serve with sour cream.

Yield: 6 servings
Preparation time: 30 minutes

CHEESE NACHOS

Ingredients:

1 (8-ounce) package tortilla chips
1 cup Cheddar cheese, shredded
1 cup Monterey Jack cheese, shredded
1/4 cup Jalapeño peppers, chopped
1/4 cup sour cream

Directions:

Arrange tortilla chips on a microwave-safe dish. Sprinkle with cheeses and peppers. Place on low heat for 3 minutes, rotate dish once while cooking. Serve with sour cream.

Yield: 6 servings
Preparation time: 15 minutes

CHICKEN NACHOS

Ingredients:

1 (8-ounce) package
  tortilla chips
2 cups cooked chicken,
  shredded
2 cups Cheddar cheese,
  shredded
1/4 cup Jalapeño
  peppers, chopped
1/4 cup tomato salsa

Directions:

Arrange chips on a microwave-safe serving plate. Top with chicken. Cook on HIGH for 2 minutes. Remove from microwave, sprinkle with cheese and peppers. Cook on LOW heat until cheese melts. Serve with salsa.

Yield: 6 servings
Preparation time: 30 minutes
Variation: Use 2 cups cooked turkey in place of chicken.

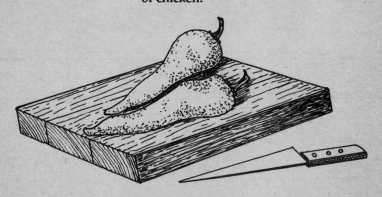

CHILE CON QUESO

Ingredients:

1 pound Cheddar
  cheese, cubed
1 pound Monterey Jack
  cheese, cubed
1 medium tomato,
  chopped
1/4 cup Jalapeño
  peppers, chopped
1/4 cup milk
2 cups tortilla chips

Directions:

Combine cheeses, tomatoes, peppers and milk in a 2-quart microwave-safe casserole dish. Cook on HIGH for 8 minutes or until cheese melts, stirring several times while cooking. Stir thoroughly before serving. Serve immediately with tortilla chips.

Yield: 4 cups
Preparation time: 20 minutes

COCKTAIL TURKEY MEATBALLS

Ingredients:
- 1 pound ground turkey
- 1 medium onion, minced
- 1 clove garlic, minced
- 1 teaspoon Dijon-style mustard
- 2 egg whites
- 1/4 cup bread crumbs

Directions:

Combine turkey, onion, garlic, mustard, egg whites and bread crumbs in a medium-sized mixing bowl. Mix well. Shape into 1 1/2-inch meatballs. Place 18 turkey meatballs on a microwave-safe plate, keeping close to the edges. Cover with waxed paper. Cook on HIGH for 7 minutes or until turkey is fully cooked. Repeat with the remaining turkey meat balls. Serve with toothpicks.

Yield: 3 dozen turkey balls
Preparation time: 30 minutes

HOT CHOCOLATE

Ingredients:
- 3 cups milk
- 1/4 cup cocoa
- 3 tablespoons sugar
- 1/4 cup whipped cream
- 1 teaspoon cinnamon

Directions:

Combine milk, cocoa and sugar, mix well in a microwave-safe dish. Cook on high 3 minutes until hot, stirring once during cooking time. Pour into 4 warm mugs. Top with whipped cream and cinnamon. Serve immediately.

Yield: 4 servings
Preparation time: 15 minutes

HOT SEAFOOD DIP

Ingredients:
- 1 (4-ounce) package cream cheese
- 1/2 cup cottage cheese
- 1 (6 1/2-ounce) can crab meat, drained
- 1 (6 1/2 -ounce) can shrimp, drained
- 2 tablespoons onion, minced
- 1 tablespoon Dijon-style mustard
- 1 teaspoon Worcestershire sauce

Directions:
Combine cream cheese, cottage cheese, crab meat, shrimp, onion, mustard, Worcestershire sauce and garlic in a 1-quart microwave-safe casserole dish. Mix well. Cover and cook for 4 minutes or until warm, stirring a few times. Remove from microwave, stir. Serve with crackers or vegetable crudités.

Yield: 2 cups
Preparation time: 15 minutes

HOT SPICED TEA

Ingredients:
- 4 cups water
- 1/4 cup sugar
- 1/2 cup lemon juice, freshly squeezed
- 1 teaspoon cinnamon
- 1 teaspoon nutmeg
- 4 tea bags

Directions:
Combine water, sugar, lemon juice, cinnamon and nutmeg in a 2-quart microwave-safe dish. Heat on HIGH setting until boiling, about 3 minutes. Remove and add tea bags, let sit for 2 minutes or until tea is the desired strength.

Yield: 4 servings
Preparation time: 20 minutes

HOT WINE

Ingredients:

1 quart red wine
2 teaspoons sugar
1 teaspoon nutmeg
1 teaspoon cinnamon

Directions:

Combine wine, sugar, nutmeg and cinnamon in a 2-quart microwave-safe casserole dish. Heat on defrost setting or on low, until warm, about 10 minutes. Do not boil.

Yield: 4 servings
Preparation time: 30 minutes

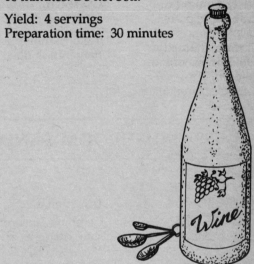

SPICED CIDER

Ingredients:

1 quart apple cider
2 tablespoons brown sugar
1 teaspoon cinnamon
1/2 teaspoon nutmeg
1/2 teaspoon whole cloves

Directions:

Combine cider, brown sugar, cinnamon, nutmeg and cloves in a 2-quart microwave-safe casserole dish. Cook on MEDIUM for 10 minutes or until hot. Remove cloves. Serve hot.

Yield: 4 servings
Preparation time: 30 minutes

MINI PIZZAS

Ingredients:

3 English muffins, split in half
1/2 cup prepared spaghetti sauce
1/2 cup pepperoni, sliced
1/2 cup mozzarella cheese, shredded
1/4 cup Parmesan cheese, shredded

Directions:

Place English muffins on a microwave-safe dish, cut side up. Top with 2 tablespoons spaghetti sauce and sprinkle with pepperoni and cheese. Cover with waxed paper. Microwave on LOW setting for 3 minutes or until cheese melts.

Yield: 6 mini pizzas
Preparation time: 15 minutes

MUSHROOM SANDWICHES

Ingredients:

1/2 cup cooked mushrooms, finely sliced
2 tablespoons onion, minced
1/4 cup mayonnaise
1/4 cup sour cream
8 slices bread, toasted

Directions:

Combine mushrooms, onion, mayonnaise and sour cream in a medium-sized mixing bowl. Mix well. Place 4 slices of bread on a microwave-safe plate, spread 1/4 cup mushroom mixture on bread. Top with the other slice of bread. Cut into 4 equal portions. Cover with waxed paper. Cook on HIGH for 2 minutes or until filling is thoroughly heated.

Yield: 16 sandwiches
Preparation time: 20 minutes

POTATO SKINS

Ingredients:

2 medium baking
   potatoes, skins on
2 slices bacon
1/2 cup Cheddar cheese,
   shredded
1/4 cup scallions
1/4 cup sour cream

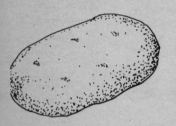

Directions:

Wash potatoes and pierce several times with a fork. Wrap in paper towels. Microwave for 8 minutes or until potato is tender, rotating once. Remove from microwave and set aside. Place bacon slices between 2 paper towels on a microwave-safe dish and cook on HIGH for 3 minutes or until bacon is thoroughly cooked. Let cool. Crumble bacon into small pieces. Cut potatoes in half lengthwise, scoop out pulp (leave about 1/4 inch), save pulp for Twice Baked Potatoes (page 46). Cut potato skins in half horizontally and place on a microwave-safe plate. Sprinkle with Cheddar cheese, bacon and scallions. Cover with waxed paper, microwave on LOW for 2 minutes or until cheese melts.

Yield: 8 servings
Preparation time: 40 minutes

QUESADILLAS

Ingredients:

4 flour tortillas
2 cups Cheddar cheese,
   shredded
1/4 cup scallions
1/4 cup black olives,
   chopped

Directions:

Place flour tortillas between layers of paper towels. Microwave on high for 30 seconds. Place tortillas on a large microwave-safe serving plate or 2 smaller serving plates. Sprinkle one half of the tortilla with cheese, scallions and black olives. Fold the other half over the cheese mixture. Repeat with all 4 tortillas. Microwave on HIGH for 2 minutes or until cheese is melted. Remove from oven and cut into 4 equal pieces, or serve whole.

Yield: 16 servings
Preparation time: 20 minutes

STUFFED MUSHROOMS

Ingredients:

12 large stuffing
   mushrooms
1 (6 1/2-ounce) can crab
   meat
1 (4-ounce) package
   cream cheese
1/4 cup Parmesan
   cheese, shredded

Directions:

Remove stems from mushrooms and discard. Place mushrooms on a microwave-safe plate. Combine crab meat, cream cheese and Parmesan cheese in a medium-sized mixing bowl. Mix well. Stuff mushrooms with cream cheese filling. Cover with waxed paper. Microwave on HIGH for 4 minutes, rotating plate 1/4 turn halfway. Serve immediately.

Yield: 12 mushrooms
Preparation time: 20 minutes

VEGGIE DIP

Ingredients:

1 pound fresh spinach,
   washed and drained
1/2 pound fresh peas
1/2 pound fresh corn
1/4 cup onion, minced
1 tablespoon fresh dill
   or 1 teaspoon dried
   dill
1 cup mayonnaise
1 cup sour cream

Directions:

Remove tough stems from spinach and drain. Place spinach in a 1-quart microwave-safe dish. Cover. Cook on HIGH for 8 minutes or until tender and drain. Remove from microwave and let sit for 2 minutes. Set aside to cool. Shell peas. Combine peas and corn in 2-quart casserole dish, add 1/4 cup water. Cover. Cook on HIGH for 8 minutes or until tender. Remove from microwave and let sit for 2 minutes. Set aside to cool. Combine dill, mayonnaise and sour cream in a medium-sized serving bowl. Mix well. Add spinach and vegetables, mixing thoroughly. Cover and refrigerate for 2 hours. Serve with vegetable crudités or crackers.

Yield: 2 1/2 cups
Preparation time: 2 1/2 hours

APPLE-NUT MUFFINS

Ingredients:

2 cups flour
1/4 cup sugar
2 teaspoons baking powder
1 egg
1/4 cup milk
1/4 cup mayonnaise
1 cup chopped apples, peeled
1/4 cup chopped walnuts

Directions:

Line 12-muffin microwave muffin tin with paper muffin liners or use custard cups lined with muffin papers. Combine flour, sugar and baking powder in a medium-sized mixing bowl. Mix well. Combine egg, milk and mayonnaise in a small mixing bowl. Mix well. Pour liquid ingredients into dry ingredients and mix until just moist. Fold in apples and walnuts. Spoon into muffins tins, filling 3/4 full. Cook on HIGH for 3 minutes, turning once while cooking. Remove from microwave and let cool on wire rack.

Yield: 12 muffins
Preparation time: 15 minutes

BACON AND EGGS

Ingredients:

2 slices bacon
4 eggs
3 tablespoons milk
2 teaspoons margarine

Directions:

Place bacon between 2 pieces of paper towels on a microwave-safe plate. Cook on HIGH for 2 minutes or until bacon is thoroughly cooked. Crumble bacon. Break eggs into a microwave-safe dish. Add milk and mix well. Add margarine and bacon and mix well. Cover with waxed paper, cook on HIGH for 2 minutes or until the right consistency. Remove from microwave, serve immediately.

Yield: 2 servings
Preparation time: 15 minutes

BLUEBERRY MUFFINS

Ingredients:

2 cups flour
1/4 cup sugar
2 teaspoons baking powder
1 egg
1/4 cup milk
1/4 cup mayonnaise
1 cup blueberries, fresh or frozen

Directions:

Line 12-muffin microwave muffin tin with paper muffin liners, or use custard cups lined with muffin papers. Combine flour, sugar and baking powder in a medium-sized mixing bowl. Mix well. Combine egg, milk and mayonnaise in a small mixing bowl. Mix well. Pour liquid ingredients into dry ingredients and mix until just moist. Fold in blueberries, mixing slightly. Spoon batter into muffins tins, filling 3/4 full. Cook on HIGH for 3 minutes, turning once while cooking. Remove from microwave and let cool on wire rack.

Yield: 12 muffins
Preparation time: 15 minutes

CHEESY EGGS

Ingredients:

4 eggs
3 tablespoons milk
3 teaspoons margarine
2 tablespoons Cheddar cheese, shredded
2 tablespoons Swiss cheese, shredded

Directions:

Break eggs into a microwave-safe mixing bowl. Add milk and mix well. Add margarine and cheeses. Cover with waxed paper, stirring once during cooking. Serve immediately.

Yield: 2 servings
Preparation time: 15 minutes

HAM AND CHEESE OMELET

Ingredients:

3 eggs
3 tablespoons milk
3 teaspoons margarine
2 ounces cooked ham, sliced
1/4 cup Swiss cheese, shredded

Directions:

Break eggs into a microwave-safe mixing bowl. Add milk and mix well. Add margarine and place in a 1-quart shallow baking dish. Cover with wax paper and cook on MEDIUM-HIGH for 2 minutes or until eggs are set. Remove from oven, add ham and cheese to one side of the omelet. Cover with waxed paper and cook on MEDIUM-HIGH until eggs are cooked and cheese is melted. Fold the plain side of the omelet over the ham and cheese. Place on serving dish.

Yield: 1 omelet
Preparation time: 15 minutes

SCRAMBLED EGGS

Ingredients:

2 eggs
2 tablespoons milk
2 teaspoons margarine
1/2 teaspoon salt
1/4 teaspoon pepper

Directions:

Break eggs into a microwave-safe bowl. Add milk and mix well with a fork. Add margarine. Cover with waxed paper and cook on HIGH for 2 minutes or until eggs are the desired consistency. Remove from microwave. Let stand 1 minute before serving.

Yield: 1 serving
Preparation time: 10 minutes

WESTERN CHEESY OMELET

Ingredients:

3 eggs
3 tablespoons milk
3 teaspoons melted margarine
2 tablespoons onion, minced
2 tablespoons green pepper, chopped
1/4 cup tomatoes, chopped
1/2 cup Cheddar cheese, shredded

Directions:

Break eggs into a microwave-safe mixing bowl. Add milk and mix well. Add margarine and place in a 1-quart shallow baking dish. Sprinkle with green pepper, onion and tomatoes. Cover with wax paper and cook on MEDIUM-HIGH for 2 minutes or until eggs are set. Remove from oven, add 1/4 cup cheese to one side of the omelet. Cover with waxed paper and cook on MEDIUM-HIGH until eggs are cooked and cheese is melted. Fold the plain side of the omelet over the cheese. Sprinkle with the remaining 1/4 cup cheese, cover with wax paper and cook on MEDIUM-HIGH for 40 seconds or until cheese melts.

Yield: 1 omelet
Preparation time: 15 minutes

ITALIAN OMELET

Ingredients:

3 eggs
3 tablespoons milk
3 teaspoons melted margarine
2 tablespoons onion, minced
2 tablespoons green pepper
1/4 cup pepperoni
1/4 cup mozzarella cheese, shredded
1/4 cup prepared spaghetti sauce

Directions:

Break eggs into a microwave-safe mixing bowl. Add milk and mix well. Add margarine and place in a 1-quart shallow baking dish. Sprinkle with green pepper and onion. Cover with waxed paper and cook on MEDIUM-HIGH for 2 minutes or until eggs are set. Remove from oven, add pepperoni and cheese to one side of the omelet. Cover with waxed paper and cook on MEDIUM-HIGH until eggs are cooked and cheese is melted. Fold the plain side of the omelet over the pepperoni side. Ladle spaghetti sauce over, cover and heat on HIGH for 40 seconds or until sauce is warm.

Yield: 1 omelet
Preparation time: 15 minutes

SAUSAGE MUFFIN

Ingredients:

2 patties breakfast sausage
2 eggs
2 tablespoons milk
2 teaspoons melted margarine
1 English muffin, slit open
2 slices American cheese

Directions:

Put sausage patties on a microwave-safe plate. Cover with waxed paper and cook on HIGH for 5 minutes or until completely cooked. Remove from oven and set aside. Break eggs into a microwave-safe mixing bowl. Add milk and mix well. Add margarine. Cover with waxed paper and cook on HIGH for 2 minutes or until eggs become the desired consistency. Remove from oven. Place English muffin on a microwave-safe plate. Put a sausage patty on each muffin half. Spoon eggs over sausage and top with cheese. Cover with waxed paper and cook on HIGH for 30 seconds or until cheese is melted.

Yield: 1 sandwich
Preparation time: 15 minutes

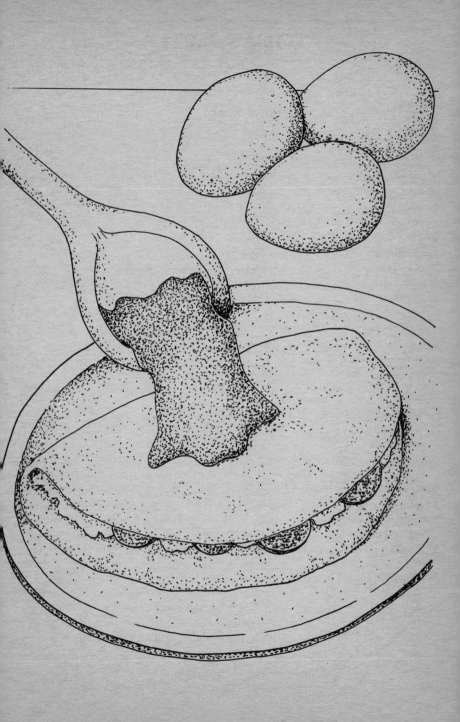

BROWNIES

Ingredients:

2 cups sugar
1 cup flour
1 cup unsweetened baking cocoa
2 teaspoons baking powder
1 cup chopped pecans
2 eggs
1/2 cup shortening

Directions:

Spray a 9 x 5 x 3-inch baking dish with no-stick cooking spray. In a medium-sized mixing bowl combine sugar, flour, cocoa, baking powder, pecans, eggs and shortening. Spread in prepared dish. Cook on MEDIUM (half power) for 8 minutes, turning once. Cook on HIGH for 2 minutes or until surface is firm to the touch. Cool.

Yield: 9 brownies
Preparation time: 20 minutes
Variation: Add 1 cup chocolate chips for a double fudge brownie.

CHEESECAKE WITH FRUIT

Ingredients:

3/4 cup graham cracker crumbs
3/4 cup sugar, divided
3 tablespoons margarine
3 tablespoons brown sugar
1 (8-ounce) package cream cheese
4 egg whites
1 teaspoon vanilla
1 cup low fat sour cream
1 cup sliced peaches
1 cup sliced strawberries
1 cup sliced bananas

Directions:

Combine graham cracker crumbs, 2 tablespoons sugar, margarine and brown sugar in a medium-sized mixing bowl. Pour into 8-inch round microwave-proof cake dish. Cook on HIGH for 2 minutes. Stir, press crumbs evenly over bottom and sides of cake dish. Combine cream cheese, egg whites, remainder of sugar and vanilla in a medium-sized mixing bowl. Mix well. Pour into prepared crust. Cook on HIGH for 8 minutes or until set in the center. Spread sour cream over filling. Cook on HIGH for 2 minutes. Cool to room temperature, cover and refrigerate for 12 hours. Top with fresh fruit.

Yield: 8 servings
Preparation time: 20 minutes

CHOCOLATE CUPCAKES

Ingredients:

1 egg
1 cup sugar
6 tablespoons vegetable oil
1/2 cup unsweetened cocoa powder
1 teaspoon vanilla
1 cup flour
2 tablespoons milk
1/4 teaspoon baking powder
1/4 teaspoon baking soda
1/2 cup powered sugar

Directions:

Add egg, sugar, oil and cocoa in a medium-sized mixing bowl. Mix until smooth. Add vanilla, flour, milk, baking powder and baking soda. Stir until smooth. Line 6 cups in a microwave-proof cupcake pan with cupcake papers or 6 glass custard cups with paper liners. Fill 1/2 full with batter. Cook on HIGH for 3 minutes or until cupcakes test done. Sprinkle with powdered sugar.

Yield: 6 cupcakes
Preparation time: 10 minutes

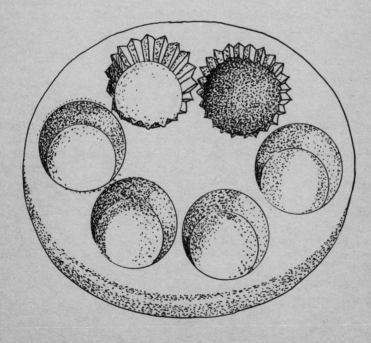

PINEAPPLE CAKE

Ingredients:

- 1 tablespoon vegetable oil
- 1 (16-ounce) can pineapple rings
- 1 1/4 cups flour
- 3/4 cup sugar
- 1 teaspoon vanilla
- 1/2 cup milk
- 1/3 cup shortening
- 1 egg
- 1 1/2 teaspoons baking powder

Directions:

Grease a 9-inch microwave-safe baking dish with vegetable oil. Place pineapple rings on the bottom of baking dish. Combine flour, sugar, vanilla, milk, shortening, egg and baking powder in a small mixing bowl. Mix well, spoon batter into cake dish. Cook on MEDIUM for 15 minutes or until cake tests done. Rotate once during cooking. Cool 3 minutes. Invert plate onto serving dish. Let stand 10 minutes. Serve warm.

Yield: 8 servings
Preparation time: 25 minutes

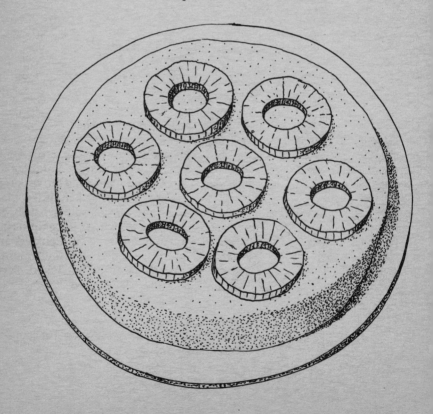

SPICED APPLESAUCE

Ingredients:

6 cooking apples, cored and sliced
2 tablespoons brown sugar
1 teaspoon cinnamon
1 teaspoon nutmeg

Directions:

Arrange apple slices in a 2-quart baking dish. Combine sugar, cinnamon and nutmeg in a small bowl. Sprinkle over apples. Cover. Cook on HIGH for 7 minutes, transfer to a blender. Blend until proper consistency.

Yield: 4 servings
Preparation time: 15 minutes

BARBECUED CHICKEN

Ingredients:

1 tablespoon margarine
1 small onion, minced
1 clove garlic, minced
1 cup catsup
1/4 cup vinegar
2 tablespoons brown sugar
1 pound boneless chicken breasts

Directions:

Melt margarine in a medium-sized microwave-proof mixing bowl. Add onion and garlic. Cover and cook on HIGH for 2 minutes, or until onion is tender. Add catsup, vinegar and brown sugar, cover and cook on HIGH for 2 minutes. Place chicken on a microwave-safe baking dish. Brush with sauce. Cover with waxed paper and cook on HIGH for 8 minutes. Turn chicken over and brush with sauce. Cook on HIGH for 9 minutes or until chicken is thoroughly cooked. Serve with the rest of the sauce.

Yield: 4 servings
Preparation time: 30 minutes
Variation: Use 1 pound boneless turkey breast in place of chicken.

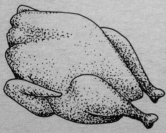

BEEF STEW

Ingredients:

2 cups cubed stew meat, uncooked
4 medium carrots, sliced
2 medium potatoes, peeled and quartered
2 stalks celery, sliced
2 medium onions, quartered
1 cup beef broth
1 teaspoon Worcestershire sauce
1 teaspoon salt
1/4 teaspoon ground pepper

Directions:

Combine beef, carrots, potatoes, celery, onions, broth, Worcestershire sauce, salt and pepper in a 2-quart casserole dish. Cover, cook on MEDIUM for 40 minutes or until vegetables are tender, stirring occasionally.

Yield: 6 servings
Preparation time: 50 minutes

BEEF STROGANOFF

Ingredients:

2 tablespoons margarine
1/2 cup onion, chopped
1 pound round steak, cut into 1-inch pieces
1/2 cup mushrooms, sliced
1 cup beef broth
1/2 cup sour cream

Directions:

Melt margarine in a 2-quart baking dish. Add onion and cook on HIGH until tender. Add round steak, mushrooms and beef broth. Cover with plastic wrap and cook for 15 minutes. Add sour cream. Cook on MEDIUM for 2 minutes. Serve over noodles or rice.

Yield: 6 servings
Preparation time: 40 minutes

CRISPY CHICKEN

Ingredients:

1/2 cup dry white wine
1 cup bread crumbs
1/4 cup Parmesan cheese
1 pound boneless
   chicken breasts

Directions:

Place wine in a small bowl. Mix bread crumbs and Parmesan cheese on a medium-sized plate. Dip chicken in wine, roll in bread crumbs. Put on a microwave-safe dish. Cover and cook on HIGH for 7 minutes. Turn over, cook on HIGH for 9 minutes or until chicken is thoroughly cooked.

Yield: 4 servings
Preparation time: 30 minutes

HONEY GLAZED RIBS

Ingredients:

1 pound boneless beef
   ribs
1 cup barbecue sauce,
   commercial or
   homemade
2 tablespoons honey
1 teaspoon hot sauce

Directions:

Cut ribs into 1 x 1 x 2-inch pieces. Place ribs in microwave-safe baking dish. Cover with plastic wrap and pierce with fork. Cook on MEDIUM for 7 minutes. Drain liquid and turn ribs over. Re-cover. Cook on MEDIUM for 8 minutes or until meat is thoroughly cooked. Drain. In a small bowl combine barbecue sauce, honey and hot sauce. Mix well. Brush ribs with barbecue sauce. Cover and cook on HIGH for 3 minutes. Let stand for 10 minutes.

Yield: 4 servings
Preparation time: 30 minutes

LEMON FISH

Ingredients:

1 pound flounder or cod fillets
2 tablespoons lemon juice
1 teaspoon dried dill
1/2 teaspoon salt
1/2 teaspoon freshly ground pepper

Directions:

Arrange fillets in a shallow baking dish. Combine lemon juice, dill, salt and pepper in a small mixing bowl. Mix well. Pour over fish and cover with plastic wrap. Cook on HIGH for 10 minutes or until fish flakes when touched with a fork.

Yield: 4 servings
Preparation time: 30 minutes

MARINATED CHICKEN BREASTS

Ingredients:

2 tablespoons lemon juice
2 tablespoons fresh parsley, chopped
1 tablespoon fresh basil, chopped
1 pound boneless chicken breasts

Directions:

Combine lemon juice, parsley and basil in a medium-sized baking dish. Mix well, add chicken, turn to coat thoroughly. Cover and place in refrigerator for 30 minutes. Cook on HIGH for 7 minutes. Turn over and cook on HIGH an additional 8 minutes or until chicken is completely cooked. Serve with vegetables.

Yield: 4 servings
Preparation time: 1 hour

PEPPERED STEAK

Ingredients:

1 pound round steak, cut into 1-inch strips
1 medium onion, sliced thin
1 teaspoon chili powder
1/2 teaspoon cumin
1 clove garlic, minced
1 medium green pepper, sliced
1 medium red pepper, sliced
1 (6 1/2-ounce) can water chestnuts, sliced

Directions:

Combine round steak, onion, chili powder, cumin and garlic in a 2-quart microwave-safe dish. Cover and cook on HIGH for 5 minutes or until steak is thoroughly cooked. Add green pepper, red pepper and water chestnuts. Cover and microwave on HIGH for 60 seconds. Serve over rice.

Yield: **4 servings**
Preparation time: 20 minutes

POT ROAST

Ingredients:

2 tablespoons flour
1 teaspoon dried mustard
1/2 teaspoon pepper
1 clove garlic, minced
1/2 cup beer
1/2 beef broth
1 boneless chuck roast, 3 pounds
1 cooking bag
3 medium potatoes, peeled and halved
2 medium carrots, sliced
3 small onions, cut in half
3 stalks celery, sliced

Directions:

Combine flour, mustard and pepper in a small mixing bowl. Mix well. Add garlic, beer and broth and mix well. Place roast in cooking bag. Pour beer mixture over roast. Add potatoes, carrots, onions and celery. Tie bag with a string. Place in a microwave-safe baking dish. Cook on HIGH for 25 minutes. Rotate dish and cook on HIGH for 25 minutes. Reduce heat to MEDIUM and cook for 20 minutes or until meat is cooked and vegetables are done.

Yield: **6 servings**
Preparation time: 1 hour

SHISH KEBABS

Ingredients:

1/4 cup white wine vinegar

2 tablespoons fresh parsley, chopped

1 clove garlic, minced

1 tablespoon oregano, chopped

1 pound round steak, cut into 1-inch cubes

1 cup mushrooms, remove stems

2 green peppers, cut into 1-inch chunks

2 onions, cut in halves

1 (16-ounce) package cherry tomatoes

Directions:

Combine vinegar, parsley, garlic and oregano in a medium-sized bowl. Mix well. Add steak, mushrooms, green peppers, onions and tomatoes. Toss lightly to coat thoroughly. Cover and refrigerate for 30 minutes. Thread steak, mushrooms, green pepper, onions and tomatoes on wooden skewers. Arrange on a microwave-safe dish in spoke fashion. Cook on HIGH for 5 minutes, rotate dish and cook on HIGH an additional 5 minutes. Let stand for 5 minutes.

Yield: 6 servings
Preparation time: 45 minutes
Variation: Use 1 pound boneless chicken breast, cut into 1-inch cubes.

SPINACH STUFFED FISH FILLETS

Ingredients:

1 (10-ounce) package frozen chopped spinach, thawed

2 tablespoons margarine

1/4 cup onions, minced

1/2 cup bread crumbs

1/4 cup Parmesan cheese, freshly grated

2 pounds flounder fillets

1 teaspoon paprika

Directions:

Cook spinach according to package directions. Drain. Combine margarine, onions, spinach in a medium-sized microwave-safe mixing bowl. Cook on HIGH for 3 minutes or until onion is tender. Add bread crumbs and cheese. Rinse and dry fillets. Place bread crumb mixture on fillets. Roll fillets, seam side down. Place in a microwave-safe baking dish. Cover with plastic. Cook on HIGH for 20 minutes or until fish is thoroughly cooked. Sprinkle with paprika.

Yield: 6 servings
Preparation time: 30 minutes

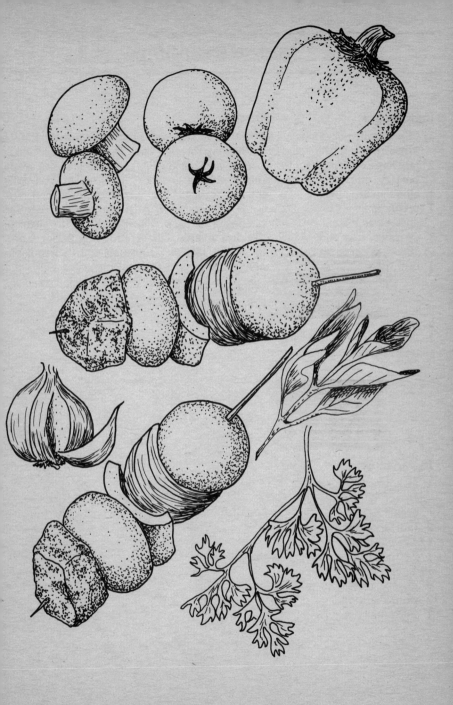

STUFFED SHRIMP

Ingredients:

- 1/4 pound raw jumbo shrimp, shelled
- 2 tablespoons margarine
- 1 cup diced cooked ham
- 2 tablespoons bread crumbs
- 1 tablespoon fresh parsley, snipped
- 1 tablespoon fresh basil, snipped

Directions:

Butterfly and de-vein shrimp by cutting almost all the way through back from tail to thick end. Loosen and remove vein. Arrange shrimp on a microwave-safe rack, cut side up and tails toward center. Melt margarine in a medium-sized mixing bowl. Add ham, bread crumbs, parsley and basil. Place stuffing on shrimp, dividing evenly. Cover with wax paper. Cook on MEDIUM for 7 minutes, until shrimp are opaque. Serve over rice.

Yield: 4 servings
Preparation time: 30 minutes

TUNA SUPREME

Ingredients:

1/2 cup uncooked elbow
macaroni
2 tablespoons margarine
1 cup celery, chopped
1 medium onion,
chopped
1 medium green pepper,
chopped
1 cup mushrooms,
chopped
3 tablespoons flour
1/4 cup Parmesan
cheese, grated
1 cup milk
1 cup ricotta cheese
2 (6 1/2-ounce) can
tuna, drained
1/2 cup French-fried
onions

Directions:

Cook macaroni according to package directions. In a medium-sized mixing bowl, melt margarine. Add celery, onion, green pepper and mushrooms. Cover with plastic wrap and cook on HIGH for 2 minutes or until vegetables are cooked. Add flour. Mix well. Next add Parmesan cheese, milk and ricotta cheese. Cook on HIGH uncovered for 5 minutes. Stir in tuna and macaroni, cook on HIGH for 6 minutes. Sprinkle with French-fried onions.

Yield: 6 servings
Preparation time: 30 minutes
Variation: Add 2 cups cooked chicken in place of tuna.

TURKEY MEAT LOAF

Ingredients:

1 pound lean ground
turkey
1 egg, slightly beaten
1 slice whole wheat
bread, crumbed
2 tablespoons onion,
minced
2 tablespoons milk
2 teaspoons
Worcestershire sauce
1 (8-ounce) can tomato
sauce
1 tablespoon brown
sugar

Directions:

Combine turkey, egg, bread, onions, milk and Worcestershire sauce in a large bowl. Mix well and add 1/4 cup tomato sauce. Place mixture in a 9 x 5 x 3-inch microwave-safe loaf dish. Cook on HIGH for 6 minutes. Rotate dish and cook an additional 5 minutes. Combine remaining tomato sauce and brown sugar. Pour over top of meat loaf, cook for 1 1/2 minutes. Serve with vegetables.

Yield: 6 servings
Preparation time: 30 minutes
Variation: Use ground beef instead of turkey, or 1/2 ground beef and 1/2 turkey.

ALL AMERICAN TURKEY BURGERS

Ingredients:

1 pound ground turkey
1 egg white
1 clove garlic, minced
4 slices American cheese
4 lettuce leaves
4 slices red onion
4 slices tomato
4 teaspoons brown mustard
4 Kaiser rolls

Directions:

Combine ground turkey, egg white and garlic in a medium-sized mixing bowl. Mix well. Shape into 4 half-inch thick patties. Place in a shallow baking dish and cover. Cook on HIGH for 7 minutes, turn turkey burgers over and cook on HIGH an additional 5 minutes, or until thoroughly cooked. Remove from microwave and set aside. Place bottoms of Kaiser rolls on a serving plate. Place turkey burger over. Top with a slice of American cheese. Place a lettuce leaf, onion slice and tomato slice on each sandwich. On Kaiser roll tops, spread a teaspoon of mustard. Place over burgers.

Yield: 4 burgers
Preparation time: 30 minutes

BACON CHEESE DOGS

Ingredients:

8 slices bacon
8 hot dogs
8 hot dog buns
1 cup Cheddar cheese, shredded

Directions:

Place bacon between 2 paper towels on a microwave-safe plate. Cook on HIGH for 5 minutes or until bacon is still soft. Remove from microwave, set aside. Place hot dogs on a microwave-safe shallow dish. Cook on HIGH for 2 minutes or until heated thoroughly. Wrap a piece of bacon around each hot dog, place in a bun. Put on a microwave-safe plate. Sprinkle with cheese. Cook on LOW for 2 minutes or until cheese is melted.

Yield: 8 sandwiches
Preparation time: 15 minutes

BEEF AND BEAN BURRITOS

Ingredients:

1 pound ground beef
1/2 cup onion, chopped
1 teaspoon cumin
1 (16-ounce) can chili hot beans
6 large flour tortillas
1 medium tomato, chopped
1 cup Cheddar cheese, shredded

Directions:

Crumble ground beef into a 1-quart microwave-safe baking dish. Add onion and cumin. Cover and cook on HIGH for 6 minutes, turning once during cooking time. Remove and add chili hot beans. Cover and cook on HIGH for 2 minutes or until beans are thoroughly heated. Remove from microwave. Place tortillas between 2 paper towels, cook on HIGH for 1 minute or until warm. Place 1/6 of the beef mixture in center of each tortilla. Sprinkle with tomatoes and cheese. Roll up, folding ends in.

Yield: 6 burritos
Preparation time: 25 minutes

CHICKEN CLUB

Ingredients:

1 pound boneless chicken breasts
2 tablespoons lemon juice
1 clove garlic, minced
4 Kaiser rolls
4 slices bacon
4 slices mozzarella cheese
4 leaves lettuce
4 slices tomato
4 teaspoons mayonnaise

Directions:

Place chicken breasts in a 6 x 9-inch microwave-safe baking dish. Combine lemon juice and garlic in a small bowl, mix well. Pour over chicken. Cover chicken and cook on HIGH for 9 minutes. Turn chicken over, cook on HIGH for 8 minutes more. Let stand 10 minutes. Place bacon between 2 pieces of paper towel on a microwave-safe plate. Cook on HIGH for 3 minutes or until bacon is cooked thoroughly. Set aside. Place Kaiser roll bottoms on a serving plate. Place a chicken breast on each roll bottom. Top each with a slice of cheese, a lettuce leaf, a tomato slice and a piece of bacon. Spread the tops of the Kaiser rolls with 1 teaspoon mayonnaise. Put sandwiches together.

Yield: 4 sandwiches
Preparation time: 30 minutes

CHEESY SCRAMBLE

Ingredients:

- 2 eggs
- 2 tablespoons milk
- 2 teaspoons margarine
- 2 tablespoons green pepper, chopped
- 2 tablespoons onion, chopped
- 1 English muffin, split
- 2 slices American cheese

Directions:

Crack eggs into a medium-sized microwave bowl. Add milk. Mix well. Add margarine, green pepper and onion. Cover with waxed paper. Cook on HIGH power for 2 minutes or until eggs are a desired consistency. Remove. Place English muffins on a microwave-safe platter, cut side up. Ladle eggs on both sides of muffin. Cover with cheese slices. Cover with wax paper and cook on LOW for 1 minute or until cheese melts.

Yield: 1 sandwich
Preparation time: 20 minutes

ENGLISH REUBENS

Ingredients:

2 English muffins, split
2 teaspoons Thousand
   Island Dressing
2 ounces corned beef,
   sliced
2 ounces Swiss cheese,
   sliced
2 ounces sauerkraut

Directions:

Place English muffins cut side up on a microwave-safe plate. Spoon Thousand Island Dressing over both sides of muffin. On both sides of muffin place 1 slice corned beef and 1/2 ounce sauerkraut, followed by 1 slice Swiss cheese. Cover with waxed paper, cook on HIGH until cheese is melted, about 2 minutes. Serve immediately.

Yield: 2 sandwiches
Preparation time: 15 minutes

HAM AND CHEESE MELT

Ingredients:

4 Kaiser rolls
8 ounces cooked ham,
   sliced
4 slices mozzarella
   cheese
4 slices Colby cheese

Directions:

Place the bottom of the Kaiser rolls on a microwave-safe plate. Place 2 ounces of ham on each bottom followed by a slice of mozzarella and Colby cheese. Put sandwiches together. Cover with waxed paper and cook on LOW until thoroughly heated and cheese is melted, about 3 minutes.

Yield: 4 sandwiches
Preparation time: 15 minutes

RYE MELTS

Ingredients:

1 pound ground beef
1/2 cup onion, chopped
1 clove garlic, minced
8 slices rye bread, toasted
4 slices American cheese
4 slices Swiss cheese

Directions:

Combine ground beef, onion and garlic in a medium-sized mixing bowl. Mix well. Shape into 4 patties, 1/2-inch thick. Place in a microwave-safe shallow baking dish. Cook on HIGH for 5 minutes. Turn patties and cook an additional 3 minutes. Remove from microwave and set aside. Place 4 slices of rye bread on a large microwave-safe plate (or 2 smaller baking plates). Put 4 slices American cheese on top of rye bread. Next place a hamburger patty, followed by Swiss cheese. Place second slice of bread on top of hamburger patties. Cover with waxed paper, cook on HIGH for 1 minute or until cheese melts.

Yield: 4 rye melts
Preparation time: 30 minutes

SLOPPY JOES

Ingredients:

1 pound ground beef
1/4 cup onion, minced
1 clove garlic, minced
1 (4-ounce) can tomato paste
1/2 cup Cheddar cheese

Directions:

Combine ground beef, onion, and garlic in a 2-quart microwave-safe casserole dish. Cover and cook on HIGH for 6 minutes or until beef is thoroughly cooked. Remove from microwave. Drain. Add tomato paste and mix well. Cover and cook on HIGH for 2 minutes. Remove from microwave. Spoon sloppy joe on the bottom of each hamburger bun. Sprinkle with cheese. Place tops of hamburger buns. Serve with French fries.

Yield: 6 sandwiches
Preparation time: 20 minutes
Variation: In place of ground beef, use ground turkey.

TACOS

Ingredients:

1 pound ground beef
1/4 cup onion, minced
1 clove garlic, minced
1 teaspoon cumin
6 taco shells
1 cup shredded lettuce
1 medium tomato, chopped
1 cup Cheddar cheese, shredded
1/4 cup sour cream

Directions:

Combine ground meat, onion, garlic and cumin in a 2-quart microwave baking dish. Cover and cook on HIGH for 6 minutes or until thoroughly cooked. Drain. Place taco shells on a microwave-safe plate. Cover with waxed paper and heat on HIGH for 1 minute or until shells are warm. Spoon 2 tablespoons beef mixture in each shell. Sprinkle with lettuce, tomato and cheese. Serve with sour cream.

Yield: 6 tacos
Preparation time: 20 minutes
Variation: Use 2 cups cooked shredded chicken or turkey. Reduce cooking time to 3 minutes or until chicken or turkey is thoroughly heated.

TOMATO, BACON AND CHEESE

Ingredients:

4 slices of bacon
4 slices whole wheat bread, toasted
2 slices Cheddar cheese
2 slices tomato
2 teaspoons mayonnaise

Directions:

Place bacon between 2 pieces of paper towel on a microwave-safe plate. Cook on HIGH for 3 minutes or until bacon is thoroughly cooked. Remove from oven, set aside. Place 2 pieces bread on a microwave-safe plate. Place 1 cheese slice on each followed by a tomato slice and 2 slices bacon. Cover with waxed paper and microwave on LOW until cheese melts. Spread the other 2 slices of bread with 1 teaspoon mayonnaise each. Put sandwiches together.

Yield: 2 sandwiches
Preparation time: 20 minutes

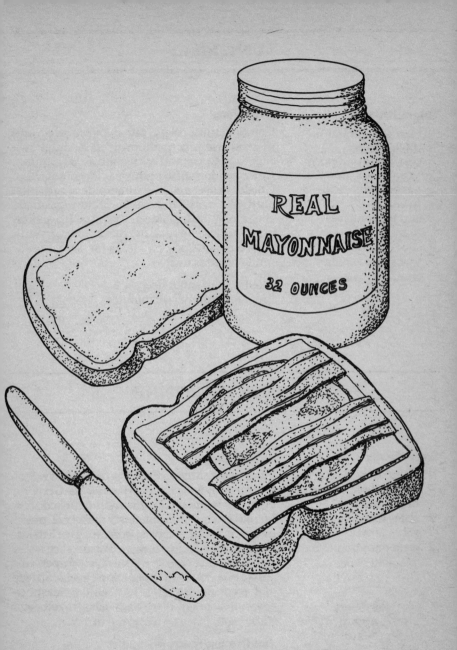

TUNA MELT

Ingredients:

1 (6 1/2-ounce) can tuna, drained
1 cup celery, chopped
1/4 cup onion, minced
2 tablespoons pickle relish
1 cup mayonnaise
2 (8-inch) pita rounds
4 slices Cheddar cheese
4 slices mozzarella cheese

Directions:

Combine tuna, celery, onion, pickle relish and mayonnaise in a medium-sized mixing bowl. Mix well. Cover and refrigerate for 30 minutes. Cut pitas in half lengthwise. Place a slice of Cheddar cheese on the bottom side of each pita. Stuff pita with tuna salad. Slide mozzarella slice along the top side of the pitas. Place pitas on a microwave-safe plate, cover with waxed paper. Cook on HIGH for 2 minutes or until cheese is melted.

Yield: 4 half sandwiches
Preparation time: 40 minutes

TURKEY ITALIENNE

Ingredients:

1 pound boneless turkey breast, sliced in 1/4-inch slices
2 tablespoons lemon juice
1/2 cup prepared spaghetti sauce
4 slices mozzarella cheese
1/4 cup Parmesan cheese, freshly grated
4 Kaiser rolls or steak rolls

Directions:

Place turkey breasts in a 6 x 9-inch baking dish. Pour lemon juice over turkey, cover. Cook on HIGH for 9 minutes. Turn turkey over and cook on HIGH for 6 additional minutes. Let stand 3 minutes. Spoon 2 tablespoons spaghetti sauce over each turkey breast. Place a slice of mozzarella cheese over turkey breast and sprinkle each with Parmesan cheese. Cover and cook on HIGH 1 1/2 minutes or until cheese is melted. Place each slice turkey on a Kaiser roll. Place on a serving dish.

Yield: 4 sandwiches
Preparation time: 40 minutes

TURKEY MELT

Ingredients:

2 bacon strips
2 English muffins, split in half
2 ounces turkey breast slices
4 tomato slices
2 slices Swiss cheese
2 slices Cheddar cheese

Directions:

Place bacon between 2 pieces of paper towel on a microwave-safe plate. Cook on HIGH for 3 minutes or until bacon is cooked thoroughly. Remove from microwave and set on paper towels to drain. Place English muffin halves cut side up on a microwave-safe plate. Place 1/2 ounce turkey breast on each half. Top each English muffin with a tomato slice. Place a slice of cheese over each muffin half (2 Cheddar and 2 Swiss). Cover with waxed paper. Cook on HIGH for 2 minutes or until cheese is thoroughly melted. Remove, top with 1/2 slice bacon. Serve immediately.

Yield: 2 sandwiches
Preparation time: 15 minutes

VEGGIE MUFFINS

Ingredients:

1 cup broccoli flowerets
1 cup zucchini, sliced
1 cup cauliflower flowerets
1 medium red pepper, chopped
1/2 cup onion, chopped
1 cup mushrooms, sliced
2 English muffins
1/2 cup Parmesan cheese, freshly grated

Directions:

Combine broccoli, zucchini, cauliflower, red pepper and onions on a medium-sized microwave-safe baking dish. Add 1 tablespoon water. Cover and cook on HIGH for 5 minutes. Stir vegetables and add mushrooms, cover and cook an additional 5 minutes. Remove from microwave. Place English muffins on a microwave-safe plate, cut side up. Spoon vegetables over muffins. Sprinkle with cheese. Cover with waxed paper, cook on LOW for 1 1/2 minutes or until cheese melts.

Yield: 2 sandwiches
Preparation time: 20 minutes

→ BAKED BEANS

Ingredients:

4 slices bacon
1 (16-ounce) can navy
   beans, undrained
1 onion, minced
1/4 cup molasses
1/4 cup brown sugar
1 teaspoon prepared
   mustard
Salt and pepper to taste

Directions:

Place bacon between two paper towels on a microwave-safe plate. Cook on HIGH for 4 minutes or until bacon is fully cooked. Remove from microwave. Crumble bacon and set aside. Combine beans, bean liquid, onion, molasses, brown sugar, mustard and crumbled bacon in a 2-quart microwave-safe baking dish. Cover and microwave on HIGH for 10 minutes or until beans are thoroughly heated.

Yield: 6 servings
Preparation time: 20 minutes

BAKED POTATOES

Ingredients:

4 medium potatoes,
   scrubbed
4 teaspoons butter
4 teaspoons dried chives

Directions:

Pierce each potato several times with a fork. Wrap each potato in paper towels and place on a microwave-safe plate in a circle. Cook on HIGH for 10 minutes. Rotate plate 1/2 turn. Cook on HIGH for 10 minutes or until potatoes are tender. Let potatoes stand for 5 minutes. Cut potatoes open lengthwise and then widthwise, place 1 teaspoon butter in each. Sprinkle with chives.

Yield: 4 potatoes
Preparation time: 30 minutes

BREADED ZUCCHINI

Ingredients:

2 egg whites
1 cup bread crumbs
1/4 cup Parmesan
    cheese, grated
2 cups zucchini, sliced

Directions:

Place egg whites in a small bowl. In another bowl combine bread crumbs and Parmesan cheese. Mix well. Dip zucchini in egg whites and then into bread crumbs. Place zucchini on a microwave-safe plate. Cover with waxed paper and cook on HIGH for 10 minutes, turning once during cooking time. Serve with your favorite dip.

Yield: 4 servings
Preparation time: 20 minutes

BROCCOLI AND CHEESE

Ingredients:

1 bunch broccoli,
  chopped
2 tablespoons water
2 tablespoons margarine
2 tablespoons flour
1 cup milk
1/2 cup Parmesan
  cheese, freshly grated

Directions:

Place broccoli with 2 tablespoons water in a 2-quart microwave-safe baking dish. Cover and cook on HIGH for 8 minutes or until vegetables are tender. Remove from oven. Melt margarine in a 1-quart microwave-safe baking dish. Add flour and mix well. Stir in milk and cook uncovered on HIGH for 2 minutes or until mixture begins to thicken. Add cheese, mix well and cook on HIGH 1 minute. Pour over broccoli and mix well.

Yield: 4 servings
Preparation time: 20 minutes

BROCCOLI AND CHEESE STUFFED POTATOES

Ingredients:

1 (10-ounce) package
  frozen broccoli,
  thawed
4 medium potatoes,
  baked (page 46)
1/2 cup Cheddar cheese,
  shredded
2 tablespoons fresh
  parsley

Directions:

Place broccoli in a 1-quart microwave-safe baking dish. Cover and cook on HIGH for 10 minutes or until tender. Let sit for 5 minutes. Cut potatoes open lengthwise and then width-wise. Put on a microwave-safe baking tray. Place 1/4 broccoli in each potato. Sprinkle 1/4 of the cheese in each potato. Cover with waxed paper and microwave on MEDIUM-HIGH for 2 minutes or until cheese melts. Sprinkle with parsley and serve.

Yield: 4 potatoes
Preparation time: 40 minutes
Variation: Replace Cheddar cheese with 1/4 cup Parmesan cheese.

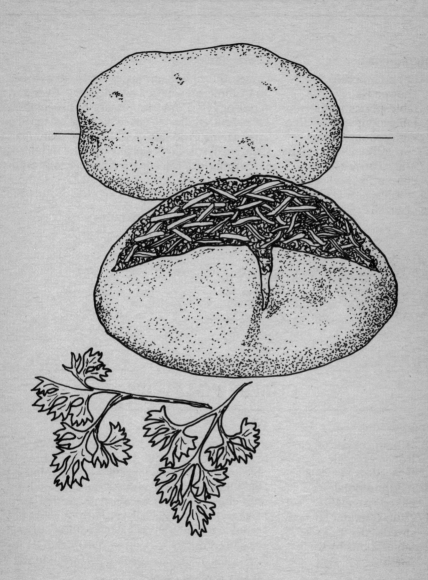

CAULIFLOWER AND BROCCOLI DIJON

Ingredients:

1 cup fresh broccoli
   flowerets
1 cup fresh cauliflower
   flowerets
2 tablespoons water
2 tablespoons margarine
2 tablespoons flour
1 cup milk
1 tablespoon Dijon
   mustard

Directions:

Place broccoli, cauliflower and water in a 2-quart microwave-safe baking dish. Cover and cook on HIGH for 9 minutes or until vegetables are tender. In 1-quart baking dish melt margarine. Add flour and mix well. Stir in milk and mustard. Cook uncovered for 2 minutes or until mixture thickens. Pour over vegetables, mix well.

Yield: 4 servings
Preparation time: 20 minutes

CHEESY POTATOES

Ingredients:

1 (16-ounce) package
   hash browns
1 medium onion,
   minced
1 (10 3/4-ounce) can
   cream of mushroom
   soup
1 cup sour cream
1 cup Cheddar cheese,
   shredded

Directions:

Place potatoes in a 2-quart microwave-safe baking dish. Cover and cook on HIGH for 10 minutes. Add onions, soup, sour cream and cheese. Cover and cook for 15 minutes or until potatoes are tender. Let stand 5 minutes before serving.

Yield: 6 servings
Preparation time: 40 minutes
Variation: Add 1 cup cooked ham, cubed, for a main dish. Use 1/2 cup Parmesan cheese and 1/2 cup mozzarella cheese for a stronger flavor.

CORN ON THE COB

Ingredients:

2 tablespoons melted butter
1 tablespoon parsley
4 ears corn, with husks

Directions:

Melt margarine in a small microwave-safe mixing bowl. Add parsley. Carefully strip back husk, remove the silk from the corn. Brush with butter. Pull husks back into place. Cook on HIGH 10 minutes, turning once. Let stand for 5 minutes.

Yield: 4 servings
Preparation time: 20 minutes

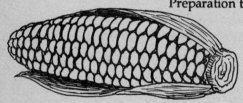

CREAMY VEGETABLES

Ingredients:

1 cup broccoli flowerets
1 cup carrots, sliced
1 cup asparagus tips
1 tablespoon water
1/2 cup mayonnaise
1 teaspoon prepared mustard
1 tablespoon sour cream
1/4 cup Cheddar cheese, shredded
1/4 cup Swiss cheese, shredded

Directions:

Place broccoli, carrots, asparagus and water in a 2-quart microwave-safe baking dish. Cover and cook on HIGH for 8 minutes or until vegetables are tender. Remove from oven. Combine mayonnaise, mustard, sour cream and cheeses in a small bowl. Add to vegetable mixture and mix well. Cover and microwave on HIGH for 2 minutes or until thoroughly heated. Let stand 5 minutes.

Yield: 6 servings
Preparation time: 20 minutes

GREEN BEAN CASSEROLE

Ingredients:

1 pound fresh green beans, tips cut off
1/4 cup onion, minced
1 tablespoon water
1 (10 3/4-ounce) can cream of mushroom soup
1/2 cup French-fried onions

Directions:

Combine green beans, onions and 1 tablespoon water in a 2-quart microwave-safe baking dish. Cover and cook on HIGH for 8 minutes or until beans are tender. Remove from oven and add cream of mushroom soup. Mix well. Cover and cook on HIGH for 3 minutes or until thoroughly heated. Remove from oven, let sit for 5 minutes. Sprinkle with French-fried onions.

Yield: 4 servings
Preparation time: 25 minutes

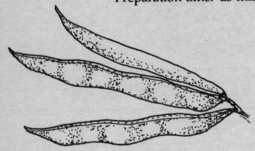

HAM AND CHEESE POTATOES

Ingredients:

4 medium potatoes, baked (page 46)
4 ounces cooked ham, shredded
1/2 cup American cheese, shredded
2 tablespoons fresh parsley, chopped

Directions:

Cut potatoes open lengthwise and widthwise. Put on a microwave-safe baking tray. Place 1/4 of ham in each potato. Sprinkle 1/4 of the cheese in each potato. Cover with waxed paper and microwave on MEDIUM-HIGH for 2 minutes or until cheese melts. Sprinkle with parsley and serve.

Yield: 4 potatoes
Preparation time: 40 minutes

HERBED VEGETABLES

Ingredients:

1   cup zucchini, sliced
1   cup fresh cauliflower
     flowerets
1   cup green beans, tips
     cut off
1   medium red pepper,
     chopped
1   tablespoon water
1/4 cup red wine vinegar
1   tablespoon fresh
     parsley, chopped
1   tablespoon fresh basil,
     chopped

Directions:

Combine zucchini, cauliflower, green beans, red pepper and water in a 2-quart microwave-safe baking dish. Cover and cook on HIGH for 8 minutes or until vegetables are tender. Remove from microwave and let sit for 5 minutes. Combine vinegar, parsley and basil in a small bowl. Mix well. Pour over vegetables and toss lightly. Serve immediately.

Yield: 4 servings
Preparation time: 20 minutes

STEAMED VEGETABLES

Ingredients:

1   cup broccoli flowerets
1   cup carrots, sliced
1   cup eggplant, cubed
2   tablespoons water
1   cup mushrooms,
     sliced

Directions:

Combine broccoli, carrots, eggplant and water in a 2-quart microwave-safe baking dish. Cover and cook on HIGH for 5 minutes. Add mushrooms and cook for 5 additional minutes. Remove from microwave. Serve with butter or margarine.

Yield: 4 servings
Preparation time: 15 minutes

TOMATOES PARMESAN

Ingredients:

1 cup bread crumbs
1/2 cup Parmesan
    cheese, freshly grated
2 medium tomatoes,
    sliced

Directions:

Combine bread crumbs and Parmesan cheese in a medium-sized mixing bowl. Mix well. Place tomatoes on a microwave-safe plate. Sprinkle with bread crumb mixture. Cover with waxed paper and cook for 2 minutes on HIGH or until cheese melts. Serve immediately.

Yield: 4 servings
Preparation time: 15 minutes

TWICE BAKED POTATOES

Ingredients:

4 medium potatoes, baked (page 46)
1 cup Colby cheese, shredded
1/4 cup milk
1 teaspoon salt
1 teaspoon paprika

Directions:

Cut open potatoes lengthwise. Scoop out pulp and place in a microwave-safe mixing bowl. Add cheese, milk and salt and mix thoroughly. Cover with waxed paper and cook on HIGH for 2 minutes or until cheese is melted. Place potato mixture back into potato shells. Sprinkle with paprika.

Yield: 4 potatoes
Preparation time: 20 minutes

CHICKEN NOODLE SOUP

Ingredients:

1/2 cup onion, minced
1/2 cup celery, chopped
1/2 cup carrot, diced
1 medium potato, cubed
1/2 cup elbow macaroni, uncooked
3 cups chicken broth
2 cups cooked chicken, cubed
1/2 teaspoon salt
1/4 teaspoon pepper

Directions:

Combine onion, celery, carrots, potato, macaroni, chicken broth, chicken, salt and pepper in a 3-quart microwave casserole dish. Cover and cook on HIGH for 35 minutes, stirring every 10 minutes.

Yield: 6 servings
Preparation time: 40 minutes

FRENCH ONION SOUP

Ingredients:

2 cups onions, thinly sliced

3 tablespoons margarine

3 cups beef broth

1 tablespoon Worcestershire sauce

6 slices French bread, toasted

1/2 cup Parmesan cheese

Directions:

Combine onions and margarine in a 3-quart casserole dish. Cover and cook on HIGH for 10 minutes or until onions are fully cooked. Remove from oven. Add beef broth and Worcestershire sauce. Cover and cook on HIGH for 15 minutes or until heated through. Remove from oven, set aside. Place French bread slices on microwave-safe plate. Sprinkle with cheese. Cover with waxed paper and cook on LOW for 2 minutes or until cheese melts. Ladle soup into 6 soup bowls. Float French bread atop soup. Serve immediately.

Yield: 6 servings
Preparation time: 35 minutes

CHILI

Ingredients:

1 pound ground beef
1/4 cup onion, minced
1 clove garlic, minced
1 (16-ounce) can chili hot beans
1 (16-ounce) can tomatoes
3 tablespoons chili powder
1/2 teaspoon salt

Directions:

Crumble ground beef in a 2-quart microwave-safe baking dish. Add onion and garlic. Mix well. Cover and cook on HIGH for 9 minutes, turning once while cooking. Drain. Add beans, tomatoes, chili powder and salt. Cover and cook on HIGH for 10 minutes or until chili is bubbly.

Yield: 4 servings
Preparation time: 30 minutes

MEATLESS CHILI

Ingredients:

1 tablespoon margarine
1/2 cup onion, chopped
1/2 cup green pepper, chopped
1/2 cup red pepper, chopped
1 (16-ounce) can chili hot beans, undrained
1 (16-ounce) can black beans, undrained
1 (16-ounce) can tomatoes
2 tablespoons chili powder

Directions:

Combine margarine, onion, green pepper and red pepper in a 2-quart microwave-safe baking dish. Cover and cook on HIGH for 4 minutes or until vegetables are tender. Remove from microwave. Add beans, chili powder and hot sauce. Cover and cook on HIGH for 10 minutes or until mixture is bubbly.

Yield: 4 servings
Preparation time: 20 minutes

TOMATO NOODLE SOUP

Ingredients:

1/2 cup onions, chopped
1 cup celery, chopped
1 cup carrots, diced
1 (16-ounce) can
   tomatoes, broken up
1/2 cup egg noodles,
   uncooked
3 cups beef broth
1/2 teaspoon salt
1/4 teaspoon pepper

Directions:

Combine celery, carrots, tomatoes, noodles, broth, salt and pepper in a 2-quart casserole dish. Cover and cook on HIGH for 30 minutes, stirring every 10 minutes.

Yield: 6 servings
Preparation time: 35 minutes

VEGETABLE SOUP

Ingredients:

1 cup celery, chopped
1 cup broccoli flowerets
1/2 cup onion, chopped
1 cup carrots, chopped
1 medium potato, cubed
3 cups beef broth
1/2 teaspoon salt
1/4 teaspoon pepper
1 bay leaf
1 cup mushrooms, sliced
1 medium tomato, chopped

Directions:

Combine celery, broccoli, onion, carrots, potato, beef broth, salt, pepper and bay leaf in a 3-quart microwave casserole dish. Cover and cook on HIGH for 15 minutes. Stir thoroughly. Add mushrooms and tomato. Cover and cook on HIGH for 10 additional minutes.

Yield: 6 servings
Preparation time: 30 minutes
Variation: Add 2 cups cooked beef, cubed or shredded.

BROCCOLI AND CAULIFLOWER SOUP

Ingredients:

- 1 cup broccoli flowerets
- 1 cup cauliflower flowerets
- 3 cups chicken broth
- 1 cup egg noodles, uncooked

Directions:

Combine broccoli, cauliflower, chicken broth and noodles in a 3-quart microwave-safe dish. Cover and cook on HIGH for 25 minutes, stirring every 10 minutes.

Yield: 6 servings
Preparation time: 30 minutes

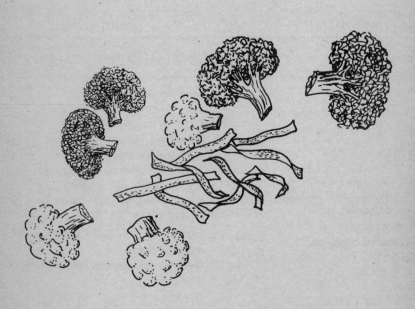

INDEX

Appetizers
Barbecued Wings, p. 4
Beany Dip, p. 5
Beef Nachos, p. 6
Cheese Nachos, p. 6
Chicken Nachos, p. 7
Chile con Queso, p. 7
Cocktail Turkey Meatballs, p. 8
Hot Chocolate, p. 8
Hot Seafood Dip, p. 10
Hot Spiced Tea, p. 10
Hot Wine, p. 11
Mini Pizzas, p. 12
Mushroom Sandwiches, p. 12
Potato Skins, p. 14
Quesadillas, p. 14
Spiced Cider, p. 11
Stuffed Mushrooms, p. 15
Veggie Dip, p. 15

Breakfast
Apple-nut Muffins, p. 16
Bacon and Eggs, p. 17
Blueberry Muffins, p. 17
Cheesy Eggs, p. 18
Ham and Cheese Omelet, p. 18
Italian Omelet, p. 20
Sausage Muffin, p. 20
Scrambled Eggs, p. 19
Western Cheesy Omelet, p. 19

Desserts
Brownies, p. 22
Cheesecake with Fruit, p. 22
Chocolate Cupcakes, p. 23
Pineapple Cake, p. 24
Spiced Applesauce, p. 25

Main Dishes
Barbecued Chicken, p. 25
Beef Stew, p. 26
Beef Stroganoff, p. 26
Crispy Chicken, p. 28
Honey Glazed Ribs, p. 28
Lemon Fish, p. 30
Marinated Chicken Breasts, p. 30
Peppered Steak, p. 31
Pot Roast, p. 31
Shish Kebabs, p. 32
Spinach Stuffed Fish Fillets, p. 32
Stuffed Shrimp, p. 34
Tuna Supreme, p. 35
Turkey Meat Loaf, p. 35

Sandwiches
All American Turkey Burgers, p. 36
Bacon Cheese Dogs, p. 36
Beef and Bean Burritos, p. 38
Cheesy Scramble, p. 39
Chicken Club, p. 38
English Reubens, p. 40
Ham and Cheese Melt, p. 40
Rye Melts, p. 41
Sloppy Joes, p. 41
Tacos, p. 42
Tomato, Bacon and Cheese, p. 42
Tuna Melt, p. 44
Turkey Italienne, p. 44
Turkey Melt, p. 45
Veggie Muffins, p. 45

Vegetables
Baked Beans, p. 46
Baked Potatoes, p. 46

Breaded Zucchini, p. 47
Broccoli and Cheese, p. 48
Broccoli and Cheese Stuffed
    Potatoes, p. 48
Cauliflower and Broccoli
    Dijon, p. 50
Cheesy Potatoes, p. 50
Corn on the Cob, p. 51
Creamy Vegetables, p. 51
Green Bean Casserole, p. 52
Ham and Cheese Potatoes, p. 52
Herbed Vegetables, p. 54
Steamed Vegetables, p. 54
Tomatoes Parmesan, p. 55
Twice Baked Potatoes, p. 56

Soups

Broccoli and Cauliflower Soup, p.
    62
Chicken Noodle Soup, p. 56
Chili, p. 58
French Onion Soup, p. 57
Meatless Chili p. 58
Tomato Noodle Soup, p. 60
Vegetable Soup, p. 61